IN THE

NATIONAL INTEREST

Sir John Monash once challenged a graduating class to 'equip yourself for life, not solely for your own benefit but for the benefit of the whole community'. We repeat this statement to our own graduating classes, to acknowledge that public good flows from education. Sir John's words lie at the heart of Monash University's founding purpose—to achieve generational social and technological transformation to meet the challenges of the age, for the aspiring communities and industries around us.

Universities have evolved since Monash was founded in 1958. They are now anchor institutions, embedded socially, culturally and economically in the communities they serve. Yet, there remains a nostalgic view of universities as disconnected from broader society—a view that continues to influence public attitudes and policymaking.

Australian universities today build and spread the knowledge acquired from research and scholarship through transformational education, working with communities, and driving further research and development that improves and saves lives. As the population has grown, Australian universities have been charged with significantly expanding education, transforming them from small, exclusive institutions into large and diverse communities. They carry considerable responsibility to drive, and pay for, the research and innovation ambitions of the nation, within funding models that are yet to comprehensively support these missions.

Australian universities are enduring and foundational pillars of society and democracy that make a crucial contribution to public debate. In the National Interest embodies Monash University's purpose by extending knowledge and encouraging informed debate about matters of great significance to Australia's future.

Professor Sharon Pickering
President and Vice-Chancellor,
Monash University

LELIA GREEN

THE DIGITAL CHILD: CREATING CONFIDENT CHILDREN

The Digital Child: Creating Confident Children

Monash University Publishing
Matheson Library Annexe
40 Exhibition Walk
Monash University
Clayton, Victoria 3800, Australia
https://publishing.monash.edu

Monash University Publishing brings to the world publications which advance the best traditions of humane and enlightened thought.

ISBN: 9781923192720 (paperback)
ISBN: 9781923192744 (ebook)

Series: In the National Interest
Editor: Greg Bain
Designer: Peter Long
Cover typesetting: Les Thomas
Typesetter: Cannon Typesetting
Proofreader: Gillian Armitage
Printed in Australia by Ligare Book Printers

A catalogue record for this book is available from the National Library of Australia.

The paper this book is printed on is in accordance with the standards of the Forest Stewardship Council®. The FSC® promotes environmentally responsible, socially beneficial and economically viable management of the world's forests.

THE DIGITAL CHILD: CREATING CONFIDENT CHILDREN

It's a wonderful wedding. The bride's six-year-old nephew and her three-year-old niece have played their parts as page boy and flower girl admirably: eager meets stagestruck. Now they settle into their seats, next to their mother, Ellen, at the end of the high table. Their supporting role in the ceremony has been followed by a round of formal photographs and I, along with the rest of the guests, wonder how they're going to last the length of the reception: through all the speeches, toasts, heckling, ribaldry.

As the best man stands to start his jocular recounting of the groom's single years, Ellen produces two tablets with headsets and gives one to each child. For the next hour or so the children are happily engrossed in their screens while the adults laugh and clap and raise glasses in response to the various toasts.

'Congratulations,' I say when I meet Ellen later, as the day moves into evening. 'That was wonderfully managed.'

She seems embarrassed. 'Oh, I'd never do that normally,' she says, almost defensively. 'I don't like to use screens as a babysitter. I'm not *that* kind of mum.'

I smile and change the subject. I had meant it as a compliment, but I had clearly touched a nerve.

I've spent a quarter of a century studying what it means to parent the digital child, and what it is to be parented *as* a digital child. Working with a range of colleagues, I've had the privilege to interview (and manage others who interview) hundreds of parents and children about their joint, and separate, experiences of digital parenting. And it worries me that so many parents feel immobilised by guilt at not doing what they see as 'a good job'. Australia's eSafety Commissioner, Julie Inman Grant, reports that while 95 per cent of caregivers in Australia say it's a significant challenge to support their child's online safety, 'only 10% of parents proactively seek out online safety information' before an adverse event occurs.[1] Maybe it's unsurprising that the only parents I come across who seem confident that they're doing 'a good job' are those who embrace hypervigilance, closely monitoring their child's digital life, restricting and controlling digital access.

The messages that parents today receive about children and screen use are alarming, and sometimes alarmist. More-liberal strategies of digital parenting can seem to offer inadequate protection against online threats, and run counter to naysaying by more restrictive parents and the attention-grabbing headlines of the latest revelations about children's digital cultures. Parents lament their lack of knowledge of the specialised digital languages used by children and teens, such as the hidden meanings behind colour-coded emojis—as highlighted in the Netflix miniseries *Adolescence* (2025), where one character explains the significance of heart emojis to his father: 'Red means love; purple, horny; yellow "I'm interested, are you interested?"; pink, "I'm interested, but not in sex"; orange, "You're going to be fine." It all has a meaning. Everything has a meaning.'[2] In their spare time, many parents are trialling every app before allowing their child to use it, reviewing their child's browser history to check the sites their child visits, reading their child's posts and vetting their digital contacts, protecting them from possible grooming, sextortion, cyberbullying, pornography, scams, sexual harassment and a hundred other concerning possibilities …

How can parents and caregivers do it all: set and enforce screen time limits, monitor what their child sees online and in the media, engage with their child's use of digital tools to complete their homework, comply with their school's Bring Your Own Device (BYOD) rules? How can they keep across what their child does online while also anticipating and protecting their child from what they might do next? And AI further complicates this picture, with recent warnings that 'we need to exercise all our mental skills – otherwise we really do risk losing them', with possible impacts on critical thinking, empathy and close relationships.[3]

Part of the problem is that the messages around technology and children are confusing. There's so much research, lots of it contradictory, while the media often focuses on amplifying scare stories: 'If You Don't Care, You'll End Up Without a Child'; 'Screen Time Robbing Toddlers of Language-Building Interactions with Parents, Study Finds'. Sometimes digital media use is blamed for stunting early language development; other times it's lauded for supporting children's vocabulary and their ability to conceptualise. Sometimes it's seen as getting in the way of person-to-person relationships; other times as a means of maintaining and deepening bonds with family and friends afar. For almost all parents, this is a recipe for uncertainty and concern—and it is leading to a 'growing culture of parent shaming'.[4] Parents like Ellen feel judged by others while fearing that whatever they do, they'll get it wrong.

In Australia, as in many other developed nations, we often promote a vigilance model for keeping children safe online. This rests on the notion that children can be kept safe by near-constant surveillance, with huge quantities of parental time and energy devoted to research into technological affordances, platforms, apps and digital device use. Sometimes this is taken up at the government level, as we have seen with the recent social media ban for children under sixteen. Yet we know that relentless surveillance is not practical, and bans rarely address the deeper problem.

Is there a way forward, through the dire warnings and the personal doubts? Do we need a policy reset that encourages parents to worry less about the conflicting expert opinions? I think so.

I believe that we should encourage parents to foster open communication with their child around digital media use, working together to develop shared protective habits while forging an atmosphere of trust so that adults can be part of a child's go-to resources as, when and if issues arise.

This book offers a revision of policy settings to help parents and governments work towards keeping children safe online—from birth until adulthood. Parents often have clear ideas soon after birth—if not before—about the kind of schooling they want for their child, whether they want a religious influence in their kid's life, what sort of diet might be best for their child and what activities they would like them to do. Very few, however, have clear ideas on how to guide their child to become a confident, competent digital media user. We need to talk more about what a responsible digital citizen looks like and how to foster it at home and at school. That's one aim of this book.

Unlike some who write books on digital parenting, often psychologists who see families in crisis, my main material is drawn from parents who are not experiencing major issues with their children's digital media use. This book incorporates insights from many parents and children who have kindly taken part in the studies I've led or worked on, primarily funded by the Australian Research Council. The parents in these studies, like all parents, struggle with which sources of advice to follow. They also have the emotional time and capacity to help with research. The findings are unlikely to benefit them directly—the nature of research means that many of their children will reach adulthood by the time meaningful conclusions can be drawn—yet they are interested in contributing to better guidance for others. They want to help everyday families juggle the rhythms and demands of daily life and digital parenting. I have been privileged to work with these families and their children, spanning in age from conception to eighteen, since 2002.

I've also chosen to refer to a range of authoritative resources that parents say they find helpful. These materials are mostly developed and supported by organisations funded by the Australian Government, or by one or other of the states' health services. This includes the Raising Children Network, which provides a suite of resources, including the *Raising Healthy Minds* app. This app provides advice on parenting from birth to age twelve, helping parents nurture 'confident, resilient children'.

This book is ideally a preparation for a style of digital parenting that centres on children, parents and family, rather than on technology, apps and prohibitions. Acknowledging that policy settings and most parenting advice tends to relate to a child's age and stage, this book follows suit.

Readers will approach this book in different ways. Parents and caregivers of a very young child can collaborate on a plan to create a supportive digital environment from early childhood. Parents of older children who have already developed digital habits may want to cherry-pick some of the strategies I've seen working in everyday families that do not necessarily get trumpeted in policy settings. Teachers and policy-makers may wish to see how these strategies could be integrated more fully into the classroom or into advice to families.

So let me take you on a journey through a child's digital life. I'll begin in utero, with their parents-to-be.

PREPARING TO PARENT DIGITALLY

Over the past generation, the path to parenthood has increasingly come to involve digital technology. Would-be parents, whether aiming to conceive 'naturally' or through assisted reproductive technology, often choose conception apps to help track hormones and menstrual cycles to identify peak fertility. Once conception is achieved, the pregnancy apps kick in. Prospective parents can log their baby's movements, along with doctor's appointments, symptoms, sleep quality, physical activity and diet.

As the pregnancy progresses, the opportunities for technological engagement expand. An increasing number of parents have 4D ultrasounds to see lifelike images of their child in utero, often billed as a 'unique bonding experience', and are sent home with a collection of images on a USB. Antenatal classes encourage prospective parents to watch videos about birth and parenting online or download checklists of what to prepare before the baby arrives. Parents may make a birth plan using one of a range of apps, or compile digital playlists for the birth.

After birth, class facilitators encourage new parents to form digital groups to check in on each other's progress and share advice about newborns. Unsurprisingly, this level of support can provide valuable reassurance, especially for first-time parents. It allows connection with others going through the same experience and, often, with health professionals who support the birth and the first few weeks of postpartum life. When someone in the community adopts an infant feeding app and finds it useful, many other parents follow suit. If someone shares a website on sleep patterns or a blog post on infant milestones, the whole group clicks and reads. Most of these parents feel they are doing the best job they can for their child—information is power, right?—until a visitor, maybe a relative or an unconstrained mother-in-law, activates a guilt trip by saying something like, 'When I was feeding my baby, I would look into their eyes, not at a screen.'

The generational tensions around parenting approaches are nothing new. But digital parenting is a relatively recent phenomenon, and we're all still a little confused about how to do it. My takeaway from the research I have read and been involved with is that families differ, as do children and family circumstances; parents are the experts in their own lives, their own families, and entitled to their own ways to parent—and that includes digitally. It would be a weird thing indeed if we recognised only 'one right way' to be a digital parent in the twenty-first century. But in the abundance of possibilities for digital parenting, there are some tips and pointers that may help some parents create the family they have always known they wanted to have.

What makes a family is a gloriously open question. What makes a digital parent is typically one or more caregivers (although some bossy siblings may operate as proxies). Whether the parenting journey is undertaken solo or in company, the transition from 'adult' to 'parent' is so great, with so many emotional, financial and social aspects to navigate, that few make significant space for conversations around digital parenting as part of the process. But as their child grows, some parents may realise that they're learning about digital parenting just a little too late. This is why it is worth thinking about it as early as possible.

For those right at the beginning of their parenting journey, the ARC Centre of Excellence for the Digital Child website, featuring research from six universities and international partners, has resources for early parenthood, including key findings from a study on parents' experiences of infant feeding and baby-tracking apps, and information about sharing children's ultrasounds and photos online.[5] The Digital Child site supports families' and children's digital journeys between birth and eight specifically. Another site, Young Children in Digital Society, while originally designed for childcare workers and early years educators, is also packed full of resources for young families.

Parents' digital media use is a crucial component of the family environment for a new child. Adults who are self-aware around their own digital media use have a headstart in becoming positive digital parents. Questions that parents might ask themselves, or each other, could go like this:

- Do we want our baby to feel that digital media is part of our daily lives, or should it be reserved for occasional use?
- What might we see as the milestones for our baby's digital future?

- How old would we like our child to be when we share a device with them?
- Do we need to tell relatives and friends *not* to gift technology to our child without checking first?
- At what age might we allow our child to have their own connected device?
- Can we set family habits in place now that will equip our baby for the rest of their childhood?
- How can we foster an environment of open communication, which will encourage our child to tell us if things go wrong online when they are older?
- What will empower our baby to grow into a confident digital child, interested and engaged in the world around them as well as in the world shown on screen?

For it won't be long before even an infant realises their parent's phone can be either or both competition and comfort. It's a rare baby who doesn't sense the importance of a screen to their parent.

This might be the time to think about what the household's mealtime rules will be. Is scrolling as you eat alright, or is there a cue at which all devices are put away or turned off, such as when everyone sits down? If you decide against making meals the time for family catchups, is there another point in the day, or several points across the week, which could serve the same purpose? As parents-to-be plan for the changes that a baby will bring to their lives, it's worthwhile trying different strategies to see how they fit. The earlier parents start experimenting with digital family time and no-tech family time, the more likely they are to find strategies that work.

The US Securities and Exchange Commission mandates the disclaimer: 'Past performance is not indicative of future results.' Each generation in a family reacts to their parents' mistakes and often seek to counter them in planning their own parenting journey. But this fast-changing world is a generation further into the digital age, and AI is proving to be yet another great disruptor. This is why the most important expertise a digital parent can have is not a deep acquaintance with technology, but knowledge of, empathy for and connection with their child.

BIRTH TO THREE

The chances are a newborn child today already has a digital persona. As a parent, your conception and pregnancy apps have diligently tracked your pregnancy and birthing, and commodified that data for use by organisations that target you with goods and services. If you've been posting images of antenatal scans on social media, even restricted to family and friends, it's likely there's a prototype profile just waiting for your child's name and date of birth. A digital footprint exists long before your child's first step.

Many parents will have a clear idea about how to best protect their children. They ensure their privacy filters are in place before they post first photos. They check they're communicating only with family and selected friends, not with the world at large, and that they're using one of the more secure digital platforms to do so. They might even start as they mean to go on, by talking with their baby about taking photos. It's a way to keep safety front of mind and model consent to the emerging toddler: the start of an evolving discussion about staying safe online. Parents might choose not to use their child's name in social media contexts, encouraging family and friends to be non-specific: 'Welcome to the world, little one.'

Parent–child digital media use in the early months might consist of watching photos and videos together, using apps, making video calls and playing music. It's amazing how half-remembered childhood ditties become clear again when there's a new baby, and once they're back in adult consciousness, the device can take a back seat as parent and child rediscover the age-old ritual of singing to each other unaccompanied. This is a stage of your child's development when it's useful to remember the long-term game plan for their digital media use. It's easy to fall into a practice of leaving an old phone to play a sequence of nursery rhymes last thing at night, for a child to fall asleep to. But it doesn't take long before the child can't fall asleep without it, and suddenly they're associating sleep with digital media in the bedroom. A pull-string or battery-operated cot mobile seems old-fashioned, but it's tried and tested.

Some parents choose not to introduce interactive media until after their child can enjoy books and turn pages. Instead, they might limit their infant's screen use to listening to music and stories with the screen off, making video calls and sharing photos with the child. Whatever a parent's decisions around a young child's access to digital media, it's never too early to start a bedtime-story ritual with a book. Although that half-hour is such a busy time of day, once they're walking and talking and moving about in the world, that special space between waking and sleeping can be a quiet time when a parent is trusted with the important events of the day. Whether it's what they had for lunch, or the latest thing that's 'not fair' at daycare, a bedtime-story ritual supports sharing at the end of a child's day. It can also spark a lifetime's love of literature.

In addition, if you're following discussions around sleep quality and wellbeing, you may already restrict or moderate your own exposure to blue-light emissions at bedtime. Supporting your child's screen-free bedtime ritual makes it easier to avoid the worst of these issues and normalises the idea that no one needs access to a phone 24/7.

I have looked for, but never found, an Australian parent who hasn't shared a screen with their very young child. The World Health Organization's recommendation for 'no screens under two' dates from a time when we were all less reliant on our phones. The few parents who say they do not allow screen time under two usually reclassify some screen-based activities as not-screentime. For instance, they exclude making video calls, playing a video of their child for both of them to watch and using their mobile to share nature sequences.

The main aim of the 'no screens under two' rule is to encourage parents to enjoy a wide variety of activities with their toddlers, indoors and out, involving both active play and quiet contemplation. Its main effect seems to be to make parents feel guilty—and, in many ways, it sets them up to fail. After all, if parents consume media often, it's normal for them to share aspects of that media with their child, no matter what the child's age. And it's not as if sharing occurs in a vacuum: there's typically lots of interaction between child and parent as a child asks for, and a parent enables, (some) screen time, as well as afterwards, when a parent asks what they liked about their screen time, and … please could they have their device back?

It's easy to avoid the cartoonish cliché of parent and child each on their own device, not communicating. At least in the early years, lending your device to your child for the time you're happy for them to be on it is one way to ensure only one of you is digitally distracted. It's around this stage that many parents become more tech-savvy, learning how to protect their devices from unauthorised use. As well as tales of multiple accidental purchases with preloaded credit authorisation, I've also heard some lovely stories of parents checking in on their pre-verbal child to find them exchanging looks, giggles and playing peek-a-boo with the grandparent they video called by randomly swiping the last contact clicked in the recent call list.

Parents who allow infants to learn the basics of swipe touchscreens can be amazed at how quickly their child catches on. Indeed, children seem to find these early digital interactions exciting and delightful, as highlighted in a 2011 YouTube video of a year-old baby who tries to turn the pages of newspapers and magazines by swiping them like a touchscreen.[6] For a very young child, touchscreen digital media can offer colour, variety and choice: sound, pictures and stories. It's a very stimulating environment and is one reason why some parents don't introduce interactive screens until they're required to, by the child's kindergarten or school.

Families from culturally and linguistically diverse backgrounds are especially likely to have family members overseas. Connecting with them through video calls is one way to promote intergenerational bonding and to prime the child for a bilingual (or multilingual) future.[7] It's further evidence of how each family is best positioned to plan their own path to a digital future. Many parents choose, instead or as well, to view videos together with their child, talking about what they're watching and, with family videos, the people the child might recognise on screen. A video of your child playing in the park, or interacting at home, can help support their language development and the naming of feelings and emotions.

Some parents use markers of book-based literacy, such as the child's ability to turn pages and to recognise the 'right' way up for a book, as a benchmark before they introduce interactive touchscreens. Whenever that journey starts, it's soon clear that even very young children have passionate interests. Whether it's trucks splashing through puddles, unicorns, dragons, dinosaurs, farm animals or sea creatures, a collaborative web search can introduce how to use media for information as well as entertainment.

It's often recommended that parents prioritise educational content for their toddlers. This can become another source of parental anxiety: which authorities should they rely on for guidance? Does educational interaction count as screen time? The fact is, at this age, everything is educational. Simply working out that Uncle Ben on a video call isn't physically in or behind the screen is a learning journey for many young children. Following a narrative story, whether a cartoon or a studio show or a fully scripted action tale, takes significant conceptual processing and a basic understanding of media conventions.[8] That's a huge achievement! And, once your child understands the format of a show and its content, and enjoys it, each episode can become predictable and soothing. Most adults allow themselves downtime, relaxing with media, and children like it, too.

Such choices and decisions reflect parents' understandings of their own digital culture and help position the child's digital media use as part of a family-based practice. A child relaxing with their chosen digital media can be a boon for parents and a great starting point for early conversations, provided it occurs alongside lots of other opportunities to develop skills, with colouring pencils, chalks and textas; with blocks and soft toys; with imaginative play such as cubbies and fairytale castles and dragons; with games of hide-and-seek and time spent outdoors. It can also help if members of the extended family—grandparents, aunts and uncles—know the basics of a child's favourite screen-based activities and how these support being in 'a happy place'. As parents have these conversations, it is also an opportunity to make their parenting plans clear to family members: they're not to offer hand-me-down technology to your child, say, or gift a tablet for a joint Christmas–birthday present, without clearing it first. Such well-meaning actions can undermine your family plan for digital media. It's important that everyone knows it's you who decides if, when and how often your child will be using connected devices.

But even the best-laid digital plan is likely to be disrupted by … the terrible twos! Regardless of when this hits—it can be before two; it can be after three—the terrible twos mark a point at which your child begins claiming autonomy. They know what they want, even if they can't explain it, and they know they want it *now*. Research with early years educators advises that 'Using social–emotional strategies such as positive language, connecting emotionally and using comforting physical contact will often resolve the tantrum.'[9]

Young children's big feelings may accompany digital media use. Even the best parent-managed transitions, with lots of warning and clear parameters ('This is the last episode of *Play School*', 'Another seven minutes of *Bluey*', 'Only until the big hand reaches twelve'), can lead to tantrums when digital media is disconnected or removed. Parents have been known to use this stage of the child's development to teach about time, and I believe this is a good idea. An analogue clock and/or a kitchen timer, set to allow the child to finish the game or the episode they're watching, gives a clear end point. Once a child gets a sense of routines and rhythms, they often manage loss and disappointment better. It helps the child to accept limits on their digital media use if they understand family routines around that use, and that technology is not always available. Some children accept that a device needs 'recharging', or a rest.

Often there's a set point in the family routine (e.g. after daycare, but before dinner, bath and bedtime) when screen use might be permitted within a semi-flexible time period. Families might use a specific device for the child's media use and put it out of sight unless it's asked for, so that brief use of the parent's mobile phone doesn't prompt an outburst when the phone is removed. The eSafety Commissioner has created a free online children's picture book, *Swoosh, Glide and Rule Number 5*, with an accompanying song and interactive resources, that can complement parental messaging around digital media use and help set the scene for a future family media plan, should a family decide to have one. It can assist a child to understand that, while they enjoy digital media, it's not always available whenever they want it. Such strategies can help children to learn about family priorities, deferred gratification and self-regulation.

It may seem too early, but this is also the time to take first steps in the long journey to help protect children against predators and sexual content online. As your child becomes interested in their body and can name their body parts, they're ready to enjoy playing 'head, shoulders, knees and toes' games with you. And they're also ready to start naming their more private body parts, which can be one way for you and them to become comfortable about the basics of sharing information about sex and sexuality together. The *Talk Soon. Talk Often.* framework, an initiative of the West Australian Department of Health, highlights how family life offers many 'teachable moments' for very young children. These opportunities include 'bath time, learning when it's OK to be nude, learning how to take care of their body and asking questions about going to the toilet'.[10] Talking with your child about what makes a safe and enjoyable online experience helps them to identify when they feel 'unsafe'. If your child talks about experiences they don't like, it's helpful to praise that awareness and show you're pleased to talk about unsettling things. Reassure young children they won't be in trouble even if they chose the action that led to a bad experience. Opening channels of communication that help you and your child share information around troubling digital content and negative experiences, in both online and offline worlds, is hugely protective. Asking questions—'What might you do if this happens again?', 'Does it feel better when you talk about it?'—builds trust and understanding.

Meanwhile, the members of the parents' group who accompanied your early parenting journey may move away, become busier or disengage digitally. There are lots of other people and organisations able to provide evidence-based parenting advice in the public interest, untouched by advertising incentives. You might subscribe to the eSafety Commissioner's Early Years program, which provides advice for online safety for children under five, for example, or bookmark *Talk Soon. Talk Often.* and the Raising Children Network sites. These latter resources are funded via state and national health budgets and draw on research from education and media specialists, among others.

But every family and every child is unique, and it's sometimes a line call as to whether an information source provides helpful advice or whether it creates doubt and uncertainty. Confidence is the way to go! Sketching a plan for a child's digital journey, as you are doing now, means you are already better prepared than most for the digital challenges ahead. Prioritising time with your child along their digital journey helps them thrive, online and off.

And, suddenly, your child is four!

FOUR TO SIX

If parents ever thought they could be the sole directors of their child's digital media use, this is the stage at which they learn that's impossible. As children become more social and go to out-of-home playdates, attend kindergarten, go for sleepovers with friends and relatives, or have babysitters looking after them at home, it becomes clearer to parents that no child lives on a digital island. Just because you don't allow images of violence in your home doesn't mean your four-year-old won't see atrocities in a news program at someone else's house.

Sometimes, seeing how other families parent digitally will prompt your child to talk about how your family uses digital media within your home. Such conversations about how your family does things and why might help your household develop a family media plan. Involving young children in this process, and asking what they would like, helps everyone feel they have a stake in the outcome. Several organisations have pointers on how best to create such a plan. For example, the Alannah & Madeline Foundation offers advice on 'becoming a screen smart family', with a downloadable family media plan template, while the eSafety Commissioner advocates for a 'family tech agreement' for under-fives and gives examples of such agreements, along with a template. Such plans all outline that children should be involved in deciding the boundaries and that any plan should apply to all members of the family, including parents.

If you do decide to implement such a plan, it's worth revisiting it regularly: not only when the plan agreement is 'broken', to remind each other of what had been agreed and why, but also to allow flexibility as circumstances change and children get older. Families may find that the most useful thing about such a plan is the opportunities it offers to discuss different ways that people use digital media. A discussion every three months or so can remove the 'Yes you did'; 'No I didn't,' dynamics and allow conversations about how the family's digital media use is changing, and why. It also permits members to talk about other approaches and expectations, such as a school's Bring Your Own Device rule or ban on smartphones, exploring how that may work, or not, for your child and their friends. The Raising Children Network has a useful video on this topic called 'A Family Technology Plan: How to Make One'.

Broader-ranging family communication practices, such as asking 'What's one good thing, one bad thing and one thing to think about?' at the end of each day also help parents and children share valuable insights. Such catch-up chats can be unsettling. Was your neighbour's sixteen-year-old cousin really watching a restricted program in front of preschoolers? What has been the impact of your child accidentally seeing a special news report on starving children? It's pointless to expect the village that's helping raise your child to abandon their own views on digital media, but talking with your child about what they see when you're not with them helps them confide in you. It gives you the chance to share how lucky we are to live where we do, in a safe part of the world, and how we still care about children and families in other places and … give money, donate food, recycle technology … whatever it is that your family does to help those less fortunate. Effectively, you're helping your child process what they've seen, empathising with others, while also providing tools to help them understand their life in a wider context.

The alternative strategy, which other parents may eventually try on you, is to call the hosting adult and ask them not to play the nightly news or any other content deemed age-inappropriate, whether that be *Call of Duty, Game of Thrones, Sex Education, Heartstopper* or anything else, while your child is in their house. This strategy risks your child being told by their friend that your call has caused trouble. It can disrupt your child's friendship network and have a chilling effect on your child sharing with you when they see things that unsettle them. In contrast, when you and your child work through these unsettling encounters together in discussion, you create a pattern of trust where your child understands you will listen to and support them without interfering, while you show confidence in your child's ability to manage challenging content, with support.

Ideally, this might also be the pattern that applies to other in-group and out-group conflicts that may impact on your child, including early experiences of bullying. While bullying behaviours in this age group are unlikely to have a technology dimension, they can set a pattern that may establish vulnerabilities that are subsequently amplified by digital media. Kids Helpline has a range of child-friendly resources for children of five and older under the topic 'Bullying is Not OK'. Looking at these resources together can help start a conversation about being friendly online and, maybe, blocking anyone who is mean to them. When your child thinks about why they should 'be nice' online and imagines how others will receive their comments, they are also laying the foundations for good digital citizenship. At the same time, accessing the Kids Helpline website together helps model digital resources as a means of getting information and support.

It's not unusual for children at this age to return from a playdate, or time at kindy, and ask you to find a game for them online or talk about a digital activity they've enjoyed with a friend. This might coincide with a period when (despite your best efforts) your child begins behaving in what may seem like an overly gendered way. It's not uncommon for children to divide into a princesses/ponies/fairies group, interested in augmented selfies with virtual makeup and tiaras, and builders/brigands/big-truck fanciers who go hunting for games featuring these elements. This is an important aspect of identity exploration and self-discovery. Once the digital gameplay door is opened, whether internet-connected or in-app restricted, it's a chance for your child to 'teach' you to play their game with them. If shared gameplay is something you can add to your family routine, maybe at weekends, it's another valuable way to connect over media co-use, with wide-ranging conversations that can be very protective in the longer run.

While you will still want to know when your child goes online, this may be the point at which you move from sharing your own device to making hand-me-down tech available for 'family use'. This watershed might sometimes be linked with a milestone, such as starting primary school. Your child will still ask for the tablet or phone, use it ideally for a comparatively limited time, and then accept it being put out of sight until it's asked for again, so it is not a constant presence in your child's life. It's not 'their' device, but it may be customised for them. It may have preloaded content, including educational apps and favourite shows, and it may be able to record videos and take pictures, but I would recommend that it not be connected to the internet while the child is using it. This 'walled garden' approach to safely corralled media engagement has much to recommend it when parenting children in these early years. It also allows you to celebrate your child's growing skills and activities, sharing in their successes when the device returns to the cupboard.

Preschool and kindergarten children are increasingly exposed to advertising in media content, whether on television, in screen-based pop-ups, or in games and via branded content. These early engagements allow parents to explain why some people and organisations pay to have their products and services advertised to 'an audience'. As children get older, such discussions can include asking how advertisers can tell that it's a good time to show a fast-food advertisement or suggest a Father's Day gift. Working with children to decode advertising and explaining why and how it exists can help children develop media literacy and, to some extent, protect them from the adverse effects of advertising. Parents will also find themselves signing terms and conditions for games, apps and other child-related services. This is an opportunity to talk about the cost of services that appear to be free, but are paid for by organisations selling users' information.

One notable risk in this age group is over-identification with the family's choice of digital/AI assistant. Whether your oracle is Siri, Alexa, Google or another digital persona, these virtual authorities can become today's child's 'imaginary friend', with the key risk age being from about three to six. While it may seem innocent that your child believes Siri is real, that belief may have long-term implications.[11] Most children will grow out of believing they have a friend waiting in the tablet or smart speaker, keen to talk about anything at any time, but this early experience of an imagined other, totally dedicated to being available, can prime the child to be more at risk from an online predator or an AI chatbot/sexbot program as they get older.

The Raising Children Network's 'Circle of Friends' activity, designed for kids aged three to fifteen, helps your child see themselves as part of a network of family and friends, surrounded by people who care about them and whom they care about. It moves outwards to include health professionals, teachers and other people your child will encounter in life, offline and on. Asking your child who they feel comfortable hugging, or getting into a car with, can highlight that it's not always appropriate to do those things with someone who is not a member of their inner circle of friends. Where an imaginary friend is in play, it might also help your child to reposition that entity as they try to work out what that friend has in common with their in-person family and friends, and what's different about the imaginary friend.

Apart from choosing not to have an access-at-all-hours digital assistant at home and asking friends and relatives to turn theirs off if your child becomes overly connected with Alexa and her ilk, another protective strategy is to ask your child everything they like about their digital friend and encourage them to see talking about friends as important. It's a common groomers' ploy to ask children to keep all interactions secret, so the experience of sharing an imaginary friendship has value. It can help to explain that you can only be certain that someone is who they say they are if you see them in everyday life, across a range of contexts. The Little Red Riding Hood folktale, with the deceptive predator the Big Bad Wolf, can offer valuable teaching points about people pretending to be someone they're not, alerting children to stranger danger online.

The 'Circle of Friends' activity can also help children explore who they are, where they come from and why they were born at this time, into their specific family. *Talk Soon. Talk Often.* offers tips for navigating conversations around relationships and sexuality while reassuring parents that they are ideally placed to address these topics. Supporting your child in their developing knowledge about sexuality helps with the long-term aim of protecting them from potential harm around sexual content online. It provides further opportunities to explain why we keep some parts of our bodies private and encourage your child to tell you if anyone shows them pictures of naked people, touches them inappropriately or wants to talk to them about their private parts.

The everyday online risks for younger children are often grouped into content (the things they might see online, including advertising), contact (the people they might meet online) and conduct (the things they might do or say online, in-app purchases and so on). These risks are magnified, or in some cases only an issue, when the child is on a connected device. Adult attention to parental controls, privacy settings, geolocation permissions, child-friendly filters and not having single-click purchasing on devices used by kids all help keep children safe, and they can also be discussed when revisiting family technology plans. Both the company that manufactured the device and the one providing your wi-fi are likely to have easy-to-follow web-based parental control and privacy guidelines to support family-friendly access. Additionally, your child's school, local library and the store that supports your device may offer in-person help. If you feel a visit would be useful, consider taking your child too, so they can see how serious you are about the possible risks associated with digital media use. Such an outing is also a means of demonstrating that people who know more about technology can often help others.

Between four and six is when most children begin school. Parents may have become used to regular updates from their childcare centre, showing their child eating, playing with friends and so on, along with the demands of preparation: could your child bring a plate to share for a Peruvian theme day, dress up as a favourite character for Children's Book Week, have a book bag for a trip to the library. Internet use may grow more frequent as children move further into primary school, as they may be connected online at school and asking to go online at home. When all days are busy days, it can be hard to prioritise genuine quality time with your child—being in the moment with them and actively building trust. Yet few things are more important. And while the best defence against online risks is co-use, another positive strategy is to corral online media use into family areas, disallowing it in private rooms.

By the time their child starts Grade One, many parents will have enabled wi-fi connectivity on a 'family' device that their child can ask to use. This allows browsing within the home—still within something of a 'walled garden' when combined with child-friendly search engines, like Kiddle and KidzSearch, and carefully curated games and activities. It's important that children know about 'personal information', when to share it and when to keep it secret: children should know not to share their full name, age, address, school and other details about their lives with strangers, online or off, but they should also understand how these personal facts can help them if they get lost in a store, for example, and need to ask an adult for help.

Children will also be learning the many ways they can access digital media. Whereas most will have already mastered touchscreen phones and tablets, as their motor skills improve, a child's keyboard and mouse skills may allow access to smart TVs, programmable robots and other connected toys. Further, as your child's speech becomes clearer, they may use voice-activated search, with multilingual children using several languages to see, for example, trucks going through puddles, often with very different footage depending on the language used. As children play together in educational settings, they develop shared interests. A schoolfriend may have learned about digital games through co-play with a sibling or parent and may want to share that activity with your child online, and you might support that.

Sitting and talking with your child about their gameplay, while they are playing and afterwards, is one way to build open communication while reducing risks to safety. Similarly, when children go online to find information, discussing what they're searching for creates a shared experience that supports skill development while building critical awareness around advertising and unexpected content. As ever, it's useful to have a range of strategies available for exploring ideas and topics. These can include looking up information together in books, as well as online; watching relevant television programs and listening to podcasts; playing games and singing rhymes. Positioning digital media use as one option in a range of fun and/or educational activities can help fuel your child's imagination and creativity.

Some parents use this age group to start experimenting with digital media access as a reward, or removing access as a punishment. One possible impact is the child values digital media even more; they may come to see it as scarce and special. Bargaining around media use as a reward or punishment sets the scene for tantrums when access ends. It also means an older child may be less willing to talk with a parent if they're experiencing bullying, image-based harassment and abuse, or sexploitation, because they worry their parent's first response will be to take the device away. So, while access to digital media may be a potent tool to alter a child's behaviour in the short term, in the long term it can have significant consequences in relation to how a child sees that access, and whether they will trust their parent to support them in a time of crisis without confiscating or restricting their media.

SEVEN TO NINE

Although policymakers, child educators and researchers talk often (and rightly so) about identifying risk and avoiding possible harm online, for most children most of the time digital spaces, along with other spaces in which they live, learn and play, are full of positive experiences. Helping your child develop a balanced appreciation of risk, safety and fun is as much about supporting the fun elements as it is about building confidence that the child can navigate any downsides.

Connected devices can range from a phone or a tablet, to a smartwatch that supports physical activity and connects with key family and friends, to toys that can be animated digitally through a screen-based interface. Children's play may include videomaking: the four- to six-year-olds' augmented selfies with sparkles and bear ears may become the full-on child recreation of a princess story. Such play is often rich, creative and collaborative: it's as much about imagination as it is about technology, and it offers wonderful opportunities for a family 'showreel', which can be shared at home first, to celebrate the skills and ideas on view, and then in private online spaces with selected family and friends.

Children often take their cues from parents' behaviours. The chances are, if you regularly post online, or use key social media platforms, your child will also be motivated to learn how to do this, possibly via an unrestricted social media channel. Building on earlier discussions, you (and your child) should generally keep posts private, always consulting other people pictured when it comes to 'sharenting', the practice of (parents) publicly sharing photos and videos. Giving children the opportunity to veto pictures they don't want posted also allows a conversation about the risks of selfie culture, even before they begin posting online themselves.

Sparing your child from the tyranny of 'likes' and comparisons with (airbrushed, AI-generated?) photos of other children might head off developing concerns about body image. Aware of changes ahead, most seven- to nine-year-olds are yet to experience puberty's power, yet playing at growing up takes on a new, preparatory relevance.

About one in eight Australian girls will experience their first period between the ages of eight and eleven,[12] sometimes well before the topic is covered in school. And, as the age of first period reduces, it is also taking longer for periods to become regular. Although children of parents who follow *Talk Soon. Talk Often.* will be prepared, this isn't true for all children. While there is a range of apps and technologies to help women and girls manage menstruation, the Luna Period Tracker for Teens, which is endorsed by several general practitioners, has been especially developed for teens and pre-teens.

Girls and boys in this age range will often play in same-sex groups with separate, usually somewhat gendered, interests: local sporting codes, musicians and musical styles, online games, fashion and dress-ups, and animals—real, prehistoric, exotic and imaginary. It's a time when your child may keenly experience a sense of rejection and alienation if they're excluded from the group they've been part of, or that they want to be in. And this is a time when some non-binary children, and children who worry that their body isn't 'normal' or that they 'don't look like everyone else', can feel especially vulnerable—assumed to be part of one group, they strongly identify with another; or they want to be part of a group but feel excluded from it.

Although cyberbullying is generally assumed to be a high-school issue, there are growing numbers of complaints to the eSafety Commissioner about cyberbullying in the eight-to-thirteen age group. While making such complaints are a last resource, when blocking the bullies and reporting them to platform operators have failed to address the issue, the Commissioner generally has 'a greater than 90% success rate in having cyberbullying and image-based abuse content removed'.[13] Noting that the incidence of cyberbullying reports closely mirrors school term times, with classroom dynamics directly feeding into online aggression, parents should be especially aware if their child seems fearful or apprehensive as a new term begins.

The eSafety Commissioner warns against disabling wi-fi or removing internet access, as 'this can actually compound the problem, making your child feel as if they're being punished and heightening their sense of social exclusion'.[14] A proactive suggestion is to work with your child to collect evidence of cyberbullying, and the Commissioner provides a handy guide on what evidence to save. AI, with its use in deepfakes and nudify apps, may well be involved in creating distressing content, so once evidence is collected, the abuse can be reported to all services and platforms where it appears. Also use in-app tools to block, delete, ignore or unfriend bullies, and if the material is not removed swiftly, report it to the eSafety Commissioner. Ask your child if they would like to talk to someone about how they feel: the Commissioner lists a range of recommended child- and parent-friendly counselling and support services. Keeping this list, or its equivalent, on the fridge or family noticeboard, and sometimes at grandparents' too, is a good idea, so the child has the information to hand. And some parents sign up for an eSafety webinar or for the eSafety newsletter.

The middle primary years is often when children begin to feel private or shy about their bodies, wanting to bathe alone and avoid communal changing rooms. They might be aware that their body, or those of their friends, is beginning to change. It's normal and perfectly understandable that children might do online research around key sexual and developmental topics online and, if they don't, the chances are that another child in their circle will do so and share the information they find. At the same time, this is the age at which some children are first sent or shown (say, in the playground) online sexual content. Seeing such images unexpectedly can be especially shocking, with much greater negative impact than when a curious child goes looking for them. The eSafety Commissioner recommends that from the time a child is eight, parents should 'talk openly about the things adults are not allowed to do with children, such as ask for nude or sexual images or videos' and 'discuss where to get help if needed'.[15]

Parents play a valuable role in identifying and challenging gender and other stereotypes, encouraging children to value kindness, think about what makes a good friend and look for people's strengths rather than focus on vulnerabilities, weaknesses or physical differences. If your child plays digital games, they may have one or more avatars. Talking with them about their avatars, and what they see as their avatar's strengths and weaknesses, can be one way to show interest in their gameplay while also referencing the different ways in which people live their lives and shine in friendship groups. As always, responding to children's questions or statements tends to be a more productive communication strategy than setting out to impart wisdom explicitly.

As well as making media, your child will encounter a wide variety of media content, at home, at school and in the homes of friends and family. They may also have opportunities to experience virtual reality and associated immersive technologies, such as mixed-wearable haptics, which simulate touch. These technologies can be very confusing for primary-school-aged children, even when an older sibling or relative demonstrates their use. Further, your child may not know or understand who else might be operating in that digital environment. Again, I suggest the eSafety Commissioner: the gift guide covers a range of tech products for children and young people with suggestions around age appropriateness, including which technology has parental controls. As with smartphones and tablets, no one should gift a child digital technology without checking with the parents first.

Conversations about challenging images and issues can occur at any time, not just in relation to digital activities, but also due to content on television, at the cinema, in print media and on advertising billboards. As your child becomes more aware of others, and more skilled in empathy, thinking about others' feelings, they can become increasingly distressed by images of suffering, including in animals, and by mainstream media programs, such as the news.

Prior to the under-sixteen social media ban, three in four children had accessed an online service (social media and/or a messaging platform) by the time they were eight, while 20 per cent of eight-year-olds had their own account, often created with the help of a parent or sibling. Parents should aim to be consistent in their messaging before and after the social media ban. When the external environment is changing, it is crucial to maintain a child's trust and understanding of family practices around media use. Reassure them that you are supportive of them, and of your family's arrangements, especially if they are working well. Older children are likely to experiment with workarounds, including VPNs (especially risky if they're 'free'), and using alternative, and sometimes less reputable, platforms. Such strategies will percolate to younger age groups. Co-watching media and open communication remain your child's best protection against these threats, enabling reassurance and follow-up discussions.

Organisations working to protect children online often have targeted messaging designed for middle-primary students. One example is eSafety Kids' 'I Want Help with Being Safe Online'. This provides a set of ten safe practices for kids that could be discussed, for instance, at a family technology plan meeting. Other eSafety Kids' resources include helping children understand 'How Do I Know if I Have Been Mean to Others Online?' Although it may be tempting to incentivise your child to work their way through the entire set of eSafety offerings, it's better to look for 'teachable moments' and incorporate the resources that way.

Moving from home to school, the eSmart Digital Licence+ program, developed by the Alannah & Madeline Foundation, has tailored lesson plans from age four upwards to build digital intelligence, culminating in a 'digital licence'. Funded by the Australian Government and aligned with the national curriculum, it is free for Australian schools and is also available in New Zealand, the Philippines and Indonesia. Across the primary-school years, the focus is on navigating the '4Cs of online safety'. Whereas the Content, Contact and

Conduct align, more or less, with the three Cs discussed in the four-to-six age group, the fourth C is Compulsion: 'This risk area encourages learners to find a healthy balance between their digital engagement and offline activities.'[16] The Alannah & Madeline Foundation also offers eSmart information for parents and caregivers to help them support their child's progress.

While many parents might feel that this age group is 'too young' for conversations around sexting and pornography, child-health professionals and teenagers both indicate that this is when such conversations should begin. West Australian teenagers (aged eleven to seventeen) suggested in a recent interview-based study that parents generally left it too late to warn them about online sexual content: most teens 'received their first [sexual] image somewhere between 10 and 13 years old'. Seraphina, thirteen, said 'it was a bit traumatising [at first] but now it's alright because it's just, like, normal'.[17] These teens say that the best time for parents to discuss these issues is before puberty, when the conversation is less likely to be embarrassing.

eSafety Kids has a self-paced sequence to help children determine what to do when 'Someone is Contacting Me and I Don't Want Them To', offering tips on how a child might respond when digital messages make them feel uncomfortable, embarrassed or unsafe. While many children may not have their own connected devices at this age, some will, and those children are likely to share texts (especially inappropriate ones) with friends as part of managing the experience and thinking through how to respond. And it's not as if the person sending the text, or sext, is always an adult: it might be the twelve-year-old friend of someone's older brother …

Children rarely use 'sexting' as a term. They talk instead about nudes and dick pics. And targeted images may be sent and received via online games, emails and weblinks, as well as by text messages. Most children won't experience targeted sexting until later in primary school or in the early years of secondary school, and a lucky few will never experience it at all, but the rumours and conversations about it often start much sooner than the sexts themselves. The Raising Children Network has a resource called 'How to Talk with Children About Sexting' aimed at parents of children aged six to eleven. They suggest that parents explain what sexting is, that it's not something kids should do, why some images and comments are inappropriate, and why if a child receives a sext, they should avoid sharing the images. Talking in hypotheticals—'What would you do if someone sent a nude of your friend?'—allows your child to explore the ethics of supporting others, seeing the relative betrayals of trust and inappropriate behaviour in the various scenarios that can (and sometimes do) occur when it comes to sexting.

The Raising Children Network also offers advice on talking with children about pornography, which it advocates doing at seven to eight years old. That's because some younger children come across pornography by accident: by clicking a link, responding to a pop-up, or using an ambiguous search term in a browser without a filter. Less frequently, children may be sent sexually explicit materials deliberately. We have yet to see the full impact of AI on this age group, but fabricated images designed to shock or astonish will also be circulating between friends, creating doubt about what is and isn't real.

As with the old April Fool prank about spaghetti growing on trees, children can learn to be sceptical, checking something twice before believing that what they see is 'real'. Playing with AI tools—to create an animated unicorn, for example—will help children understand the role of the prompt. It's also worth talking to children about the energy and environmental costs that underpin even small AI queries, indicating that what looks simple is actually complicated and costly. If there's a parent-and-child workshop on AI to attend, so much the better. The ARC Centre of Excellence for the Digital Child website has a report for parents of younger children, 'Children and Generative AI (GenAI) in Australia: The Big Challenges', that can be used to discuss AI.[18] As well as featuring beautiful but weird, error-laden AI-created images to which a child can respond, such as a shiny calculator with a keyboard with three separate keys marked '2', the report calls for 'critical AI literacies' that encourage children to question whether they want to use AI, given its costs and biases.

Returning to children's first encounters with sexual images, AI-generated or otherwise, this is where again a tradition of 'checking in' on one good thing, one bad thing and one thing to think about can be extremely helpful. This reflective space may start a conversation about 'growing up', or the way that bodies change between childhood and adulthood. Open conversations between you and your child won't stop them encountering sexual topics that might seem to be totally inappropriate, but if they're able to talk with you about these issues, they can process information more positively and check misunderstandings before they take root.

Although it's tempting to try to 'out' the child who may have forwarded sexually explicit material, such a strategy may complicate your child's life and close avenues of communication, whereas trusting that your conversations are protective, and reassuring and affirming your child's decision to talk with you about what they have seen, sends a message that you know they can handle these challenges in their own way, but you're glad they trust you with talking things over. Many experts suggest that asking a child what they have seen and how it made them feel, and explaining that pornography isn't designed for children's eyes, is the best way to protect them from its risks and harms. For parents already following the *Talk Soon. Talk Often.* framework, these sexuality-related conversations will be getting easier as they become more pertinent and necessary. At the same time, conversations started at any age are valuable and protective.

If an adult is contacting a child to ask them to send sexually explicit material, that's illegal, as well as being a red flag for grooming behaviour. The Raising Children Network advises parents in this position to contact the National Domestic Family and Sexual Violence Counselling Service, 1800 RESPECT (1800 737 732), and, if adults have reason to believe a child has been sexually abused, the police. Their 'Child Sexual Abuse: Helplines and Services' resource page also has a range of state-based services that may offer face-to-face support for you and/or your child.

A subsection of parents caring for children around this age might start checking their child's browsing history, especially after a scary incident like the child encountering pornography. They worry that a shocking first encounter with porn might prompt their child to seek it out, trying to understand it (or adults) better. No matter how good the intention, this can create a negative dynamic. A child who was trusting and open may become secretive, unwilling to share their thoughts and experiences. Parents might worry more but get told less, and find that cooperation is replaced by evasion. Your child telling you about their encounter with pornography or sexting is not a reason to change your approach to digital parenting: it's a sign that it's working. And while your child may try to find out more about what porn is and why it exists, the teens my team and I have talked to say that when they go looking for porn it's much less of a shock than seeing it unexpectedly.

For most parents, most of the time, the seven- to nine-year-old age period is the calm before the adolescent storm. Children generally accept their parents' guidance around aspects like parental controls and filters, accessing digital media in family spaces, not having connected technology in bedrooms, and leaving devices to charge in an open space overnight. While their friends are important, and they are developing passions and interests that can sustain them throughout their lives, their parents are still the people to please and look up to. And then they move into double digits: ten!

TEN TO TWELVE

Here we hit the pre-teens: the period bridging childhood and adolescence. Pre-teens can enrich their knowledge about digital media by thinking about digital citizenship. This notion entails both rights and responsibilities. Rights include using digital media in all its richness, for connection, collaboration and creativity, without others feeling hurt or excluded. Responsibilities include knowing how to be safe online, being respectful, using digital media legally and helping others feel safe too. Children become digital citizens through their activities in digital spaces. A child may be a good digital citizen or a bad one, but once they are active online they can't choose not to be a digital citizen.

Ideally, children understand that people should be as caring and considerate online as offline. Being in a virtual space does not allow people to be horrible. Basic online safety in this age group includes early conversations before there's an incident. As the eSafety Commissioner notes, discussions about 'online safety will provide your child with the social and emotional skills needed to reduce the risks and make our communities safer for all'. Sadly, ten- to twelve-year-olds are at particular risk of cyberbullying, with the Commissioner observing that their figures show 'children transitioning to secondary school accounting for more than a third of all cases'.[19]

While you might have enabled a range of safety settings on your child's device, the chances are your child can now learn to make these settings too: both to safeguard themselves and to help their friends. Some parents may worry that such skills make it easier for their child to turn off filters, open private browsers and wipe their search history. Descriptors of the how-to protocols for these actions are readily accessible through a targeted internet search, however, and the knowledge that informs conscious choice around safety is more beneficial than it is risky.

Indeed, digital citizenship involves making informed choices. It also requires children not to believe everything they see and read. Building upon earlier discussions about people online pretending to be a child when they're an adult, and about AI fakes, your child can learn to check apparent facts against a range of sources, and to identify which sites are reliable as fact-checking resources and why. Being a maturing digital citizen means checking both that people are who they say they are and that what they say is true.

Although digital citizenship includes learning about rules and regulations, and what can and can't be done appropriately online, children increasingly make their own decisions as they move through their pre-teen years. A 2025 eSafety Commissioner report, 'Behind the Screen: The Reality of Age Assurance and Social Media Access for Young Australians', found that over 80 per cent of children between eight and twelve regularly accessed social media accounts that were supposed to be for over-thirteens. While there is now a ban on Australian under-sixteens having their own account on some platforms, it's unlikely that this will stop them from using social media. Instead, it may mean that friendship groups move onto less-regulated apps not traditionally associated with teens, such as WhatsApp.

So, what are the risks and benefits of social media, and why are younger social media users of particular concern? For many pre-teens and under-sixteens, social media is a way for them to connect with the same people they spend time with offline: friends, family and classmates. It provides opportunities to explore new interests and hobbies, developing their understanding of history, geography and the world. It can foster a sense of belonging, especially for children who identify with the LGBTIQA+ community, for First Nations children, for children from a linguistic diaspora and for children who live with a disability or who are neurodiverse. As the eSafety Commissioner, Julie Inman Grant, notes, such children may 'feel more themselves in an online environment than they do in real life': 'This has served as a lifeline for them—and we certainly do not want to undermine those benefits—we want to harness them!'[20] Children who find in-person social exchange challenging often enjoy the comparative anonymity and reduced social pressure of digital exchange, finding it easier to communicate their thoughts and feelings. Responding to this, headspace, the national youth mental-health foundation, offers information for preteens and teens who feel 'upset, worried or angry' about the social media ban.[21]

The negatives of social media are principally related to the distressing and unsettling content that children might see, doomscrolling, and the risky ways in which children might behave: uploading inappropriate photos of themselves or others and/or sharing personal or private information with strangers. Some children want to increase the number of their online 'friends' and click to accept requests from people they don't know in person; others may become over-invested in collecting 'likes' online. Social media also connects young people to a range of influences and influencers, some of which are profoundly negative. Parents and online safety experts are rightly concerned about online echo chambers and their influence on children's vulnerabilities, such as around body dysmorphia or the manosphere, especially 'if that young person is already grappling with a precarious sense of self', as Grant puts it.[22]

As part of Australia's national commitment to ending violence against women and children, eSafety has produced two research-informed reports: 'Being a Young Man Online' and 'Supporting Young Men Online'. Grant notes: 'Big Tech may insist that recommender systems purely serve the content interests of the user, but we argue they're also designed to entrap vulnerable users in an endless content loop that preys on their deepest insecurities.' While regulators work to change the Big Tech operational settings, parents' listening, supporting and asking questions remains a key protection for vulnerable youth, along with the helplines on the fridge.

Whatever the platform, app or online service, banned or not, risks are magnified if your child's account settings are not well regulated and private. Lax settings can amplify the dangers associated with cyberbullying, with your child feeling at risk if they're online with one or more digital aggressors. As well as interpersonal concerns, there are commercial risks, especially from data breaches and via targeted advertising, which may be even more inappropriate if the child has given a misleading birthdate as part of setting up an account. Algorithms and other aspects of social media that keep young people (and their parents) doomscrolling can fuel fears around missing out on what's happening, while social pressure may mean that a child feels they have to respond quickly to a friend's post or risk having their silence or slowness misinterpreted.

The eSafety Commissioner argues that pre-teens and teens face an unfair fight against 'the algorithm effect'. She advocates for a policy shift to move the responsibility for safety onto the platforms through embedding Safety by Design. The eSafety Commissioner website offers guidance for industry that outlines what it would look like for Big Tech to embrace the principle of supporting families to achieve safer outcomes for young people. Until that happens, it can be protective for children to have a personal smartphone at a later age rather than a younger one, with that benefit strengthened by regular periods of digital disengagement.

If your family is one that charges phones and connected media in shared domestic space (like the kitchen) overnight, your child will be used to a night-time phone-free period and will be better primed for a restful sleep. Good sleep habits are likely to support your child to manage the stresses that come with peer group interactions, both online and off. In addition to an overnight digital detox, some families choose to share activities that take them away from home and the routine of wi-fi connectivity, whether that be cycling, boating, birdwatching, et cetera. Sometimes, weekend pursuits are augmented by digital detox holidays: camping in the bush, for example.

Shared family activities in outdoor contexts can also offset children becoming less active. As pre-teens move through their final primary years, they often navigate increased homework demands by engaging less in collaborative play with friends. This can be an opportunity to introduce activity apps and exercise smartwatches, especially if parents also use these, and tech-facilitated outdoor and movement games, such as Pokemon Go. Competitions around who walks the most steps on which days or over which weeks can help gamify physical activity for some children.

Although the Alannah & Madeline Foundation notes that one-third of Australian children aged between six and thirteen have their own phone, they also reveal that the most popular age for children to get a phone is twelve to thirteen, as they transition to secondary school. In their factsheet, 'How to Determine if Your Child Is Ready for Their Own Smartphone', the foundation recommends parents consider the child's capacity to care for the device (even if it is a hand-me-down), their level of responsibility in terms of the bills to be paid and their understanding of good practices around digital technology use, such as maintaining privacy, demonstrating respect and understanding the need to disengage. Many schoolchildren will have taken or be taking the foundation's eSmart Digital Licence+ Program, originally conceptualised as a 'digital driving licence'.

If children did not encounter sexting and pornography before they turned ten, the chances are they, or their friends, will do so by the time they are twelve. Receiving sexual images unexpectedly, whether user-generated, AI-manufactured or commercially produced, is a visual assault. An unsolicited picture of this type is often termed 'image-based sexual harassment and abuse' or 'technology-facilitated violence'. While younger children may be puzzled and repulsed, older children often feel shocked or unsafe, confronted by another person seeing them as a recipient for sexual messaging and maybe feeling punished for some innocent comment or behaviour. It's helpful to reassure the child that they are *never* responsible for what other people do, say or send them. It says nothing about them: the behaviour solely reflects on the sender.

But what if your child is the sender, the one who forwarded or shared a sext or pornography? What if, in a sense, they aren't old enough to know better? Perhaps they're an impressionable child, strung along by a more aware, manipulative one? Hopefully, the dynamics of the situation can be uncovered as the various children involved work with parents and teachers to understand what happened, why and how. If your child is in that situation, they will need support as they try to understand why they became involved in inappropriate messaging, and to help them empathise with the child or children who received the images. Talking this through with your child allows you to focus on the positive skills of caring about other people's thoughts and feelings, seeing the potential hurt and the error involved in the poor choice they made. The eSafety message to 'stop and think about any content before you post or send it' is a valuable one, as is reminding children that it helps to say sorry when you make a mistake.

While these may be tough lessons for a child confronted with choice and consequence, and while the overarching impact depends upon the wider context as well as the school's and parents' approach, the message about keeping talking, and reassuring your child to turn to trusted adults if they feel pressured, and not to do or say to others things that feel risky or hurtful, remain key to learning from the experience. At the same time, one reason why sexts and pornography have the power they do in pre-teen and teen years is that they are linked to topics often considered taboo: sex, abuse, exploitation. Adults and children can have a tough time talking together about these topics, but this is less likely when families *Talk Soon. Talk Often.*

Some children may turn to human-like AI companions because there's no risk of the chatbot rejecting or reporting them. The eSafety Commissioner found that, in early 2025, there were 'more than 100 AI companions available' and that these 'often lack[ed] mechanisms to enforce age restrictions and other safety measures'. Risks identified include exposure to dangerous concepts, dependency and social withdrawal, unhealthy attitudes to relationships, heightened risk of sexual abuse, compounded risk of bullying, and financial exploitation. As well as suggesting open communication with your child about these risks, advice to parents includes a way to support staged withdrawal from an AI companion 'relationship':

- set clear limits (boundaries are helpful, whereas an outright ban drives behaviour underground, making it more difficult for a child to confide in their parent)
- identify triggers (so the child can work through emotions that predispose them to engage with an AI companion and develop other ways to handle these)
- promote healthy alternatives (including outdoor and sporting activities)
- foster in-person connections (with family and friends)
- encourage gradual reduction (by slowly reducing AI companion time)
- teach mindfulness (there are apps to help with this, so the child can choose which app to use, or

maybe develop the practice of only accessing the AI companion after some mindful practice, such as deep breathing and meditation)
- reach out for support (for example, to one of the kids' helplines).[23]

Although Relationships and Sexuality Education is a central element of the national school curriculum, there are state- and territory-related differences in the approaches taken. These differences in educational settings are amplified by the kind of school the child attends (state school, independent school, faith-based school), the training the relevant teacher has received and the level of comfort the teacher has around the various topics to be covered. Often, complex issues that might otherwise allow deep discussions between children and their teacher, and subsequently children and their parents, may be covered by watching a brief video and completing a worksheet.

In general, the teens (and a few pre-teens) in our research tell us that the messages they receive in educational contexts around pornography, sexting and digital artefacts like AI companions is simply 'don't'. It's clear that this message isn't working. Teens, and some pre-teens, receive and send sexts, view pornography and use AI companions. Few have the opportunity for informative chats with non-judgemental adults who might help them manage the risks of the images they may create, the content they find and the conversations they are led into as they follow their curiosity and search for materials they hear about from friends.

Internet safety for pre-teens includes explaining the 'corporatisation' of digital media. This can cover data safety, and the types of terms and conditions that adults sign when accessing services. Children can also learn that advertising isn't always true, is rarely objective and is unlikely to be balanced. Like the digital content targeting your child, advertising is delivered by algorithms that respond to the ways your child uses digital media and the things that interest them. That specific dataset means your child sees advertisements that differ from the ones you see, or the ones their best friend sees. Your child might like some adverts they get: it's worth asking which ones, and why. You can explain to your child that advertising is content created for a purpose, it's usually slick and often has a large budget, and it's designed with a specific audience in mind, to promote a specific response.

Similar discussions about pornography, and the various markets for pornographic materials, responding (ideally) to questions asked by the child, can help children understand why this content is not designed for them. Such discussions may also highlight that many of the activities shown in porn are unusual, as are porn stars' bodies. It may be worth asking whether stars' bodies differ from those your child sees in a changing room, or on a beach. Talking about what your child may have seen portrayed in pornography allows you to discuss the elements of fantasy and pretence. In much the same way that advertising shows sunshine and blue skies, pornographic films show only certain aspects of sex and sexuality because that's what producers think porn audiences want.

While newly introduced age-verification measures may prevent some underage access to adult content, as well as restricting specific social media platforms, age verification is unlikely to mean that no younger teen or pre-teen ever sees porn again. Further, Burnet Institute researchers working with parents and teens found that 'both adult and adolescent participants overwhelmingly agreed that age-appropriate conversations remained the most suitable and preferred course of action for addressing concerns of online harm [such as pornography] to young people'.[24] Teens tell my research team that these conversations are best begun in primary school, to prepare them for the different dynamics of high school, and also because sexual topics are less embarrassing pre-puberty. Parental support, and children's own critical thinking skills, are valuable protections against these and myriad other online risks.

As twelve is often on or about the age at which children move to high school, it's also a positive time to support your child in continuing the friendships made during their primary years, at least with one or two children. This is especially helpful in circumstances when those primary-school friends don't move to the same secondary school as your child, or when the friendships are associated with a sporting team, church or youth group, or another out-of-school hobby. It can be protective for children to have more than one friendship circle, so that if there's chaos in one part of their social world, there can be solace, advice and support on offer from peers in another of their social circles.

THIRTEEN TO FIFTEEN

For many parents, the early teen years—from the thirteenth birthday until the sixteenth—are especially fraught, and may be characterised by their child displaying risky behaviours. It can be tempting to ramp up the kinds of protections that may have felt supportive for a younger child, such as monitoring social media posts, checking websites and enabling geolocation tracking. Yet for family members regularly checking in with each other around their family technology plan, the move to secondary school is often the point at which these protections can be scaled back. Instead, the adolescent can be asked what support they want and encouraged to suggest (reasonable) strategies that might be helpful. This recognises and affirms your child's developing autonomy while sending a signal about trust. An important added benefit of this approach is that it explicitly identifies some protective behaviours as unsuited to maturing teens and helps prepare your child to identify and resist digitally facilitated coercive control at the hands of a future romantic partner.

The thirteen-to-fifteen age range is both the eye of the adolescent storm and the key developmental stage the Australian Government targeted with the decision to make sixteen the minimum age for teens creating certain social media accounts. Previously, that age had nominally been thirteen, but apps and platforms made minimal attempts at age-based compliance. Younger children, sometimes with parental help, could tick a box or insert a false birthdate, setting up an account well before their thirteenth birthday. While this is increasingly unlikely, few thirteen- to fifteen-year-olds seem to have been excluded from their chosen social media accounts, while some adult sites have closed down all Australian access to protest the new online safety codes from the Office of the eSafety Commissioner.

The *Australian Online Safety Amendment (Social Media Minimum Age) Act* was passed in November 2024 and implemented in December 2025. In the meantime, the government expected technology companies to explore a range of fit-for-purpose measures for verifying the age of everyone opening (or holding) a social media account so that only people over sixteen could hold specified digital media accounts. Trumpeted as a world-first, the Act put the onus on Big Tech to stop under-sixteens from holding certain accounts.

It's deliberately not the parents, or the child, to be held responsible if the prohibition fails.

Notably, this Australian social media ban was not recommended in the *Report of the House of Representatives' Select Committee on Social Media and Online Safety* (2022), a major government review. While the review recommended the highest privacy and safety settings as the default for under-eighteens, the committee stopped well short of banning access for children under sixteen. Similarly, the Australian Government's *Response to the Social Media and Online Safety Report* (2023) made no mention of the legislation that was to be enacted twenty months later. Yet by June 2024 both Peter Dutton, then leader of the Opposition, and Anthony Albanese, as Prime Minister, supported banning some social media accounts for children under sixteen, and that policy was legislated in November 2024.

Few teenagers were involved in these deliberations. Instead, Melbourne teenager Leonardo Puglisi became an informal spokesperson for teens aged thirteen to sixteen, even though he fell just outside that age range himself. Leo had set up his own news channel, 6 News Australia (originally called *HMV Local News*), in 2019, when he was eleven. The ABC interviewed Leo about the proposed ban in 2024. Leo's response was nuanced. He recognised, as all inquiries have, that some people experience harm while using social media. But his argument was that harm has more to do with how specific people use social media rather than their age, and that many people find social media use to be beneficial.

The social media ban is poor policy that responds to a media-amplified techno-panic of the kind that also calls out parents for, for example, allowing children under two to use screens. It buys into the alarm that also drove Jonathan Haidt's 2024 bestseller *The Anxious Generation: How the Great Rewiring of Childhood is Causing an Epidemic of Mental Illness.* While opinion polls indicate the policy is popular with voters, children under sixteen have responded in thoughtful ways, arguing that the legislation misses the point and they want social media improved, not banned. And children are finding workarounds. One Perth thirteen-year-old retook a facial scan a short while after social media age verification correctly identified her as underage. The second time, she passed.[25]

Most nearly-sixteen-year-olds interviewed by our research team before the ban came into effect were more intrigued than worried. They were confident that, in the same way they managed to watch R-rated films, and access porn, vapes, tobacco and alcohol, they would find a way around whichever age-verification system Big Tech used. Many said they had used VPNs for years to bypass the family-friendly filters their parents had put in place. Such teens were often in favour of filters to protect younger children, but argued that once they were old enough to master the workarounds, they were old enough to engage with the content that regulators felt they should not.[26] The eSafety Commissioner says: 'We are all well aware that teens will find workarounds, just as some people speed despite speed limits or drink underage despite age restrictions. But these rules matter because they delay exposure, reduce harm, and set a clear social norm.'[27]

The driving vision behind the under-sixteen social media ban seems to be to protect teens from the digitally amplified fallout of toxic relationships with their peers, online and off. Whether that fallout comes from 'thinspiration' anorexia-promotion sites; self-harm and suicide-supporting sites; cyberbullying; image-based sexual harassment and abuse, including AI-facilitated deepfake porn; or sextortion, the social media ban buys into the trauma that sees one in two young Australians impacted by suicide (not necessarily youth suicide) by the time they turn twenty-five.[28] And while many of these sites have helplines for children, some of them, like ReachOut, also offer free online or telephone sessions to help parents support their children.

While cyberbullying is a risk factor for child suicide, the power of cyberbullying lies in the interpersonal dynamics of the teens' social circles. That's important because these are the children that teens interact with every day, at school and in their neighbourhood. In sextortion, for example, and image-based sexual harassment and abuse, it's the aggressor's threat to post images to a victim's social circle that often causes the trauma. One way to defuse that threat is to educate children about these dynamics, enabling them to frame the perpetrator as the wrongdoer, *never* the victim.

As well as enabling fast dissemination of private content to a number of people, the cyber aspect of cyberbullying includes a sense of continuous engagement, of the victim having no way to escape from the harassment, of bringing aggression and conflict into their home and safe spaces through their connected media. This is aggravated by teen victims' tendencies to stay online as drama unfolds, rather than turning the device off and walking away. Arguably, walking away is more possible if your teen is used to leaving connected media out of their bedroom. These issues are likely to be amplified by emerging AI technologies.

Available support organisations include Dolly's Dream, which was specifically set up to address bullying-related youth suicide risk, and Beyond Blue Youth Support, which is aimed at young people between the ages of twelve and twenty-five. ReachOut also offers guidance for parents on how to support children figuring out their gender identity, while the eSafety Commissioner gives specialist supports for online hate and abuse against First Nations children. The Commissioner's general reporting mechanisms and takedown powers for all cyberbully victims under eighteen also have an excellent success rate.

Tragically, there are year-on-year increases in reports of cyberbullying, 'including aggressive online behaviour by teens bordering on the mercenary and the merciless', the eSafety Commissioner reports. Growing criminal involvement in sextortion and the fear that 'manipulative chatbots will start being deployed to target younger people with even greater precision and on a more massive scale' are also key concerns. In the period from June 2023 to July 2024, the eSafety Commissioner received '7,000 reports of image-based abuse—intimate images shared without consent—including seeing deepfake and nudifying apps being used by teenagers to target their female classmates'.[29] Given these pressures and dynamics, it's not surprising that the implied driver of the recent social media ban is teen mental health and the risk of suicide.

Thus, it might seem counterintuitive to learn that the rate at which children suicide in Australia has trended lower over the past five years.[30] The 2024 figures record seventy child deaths, aged five to seventeen, of which sixty-one were in the fourteen to seventeen age range. While these are frightening numbers, and the impacts of each death upon family, friends and community cannot be overstated, the figures indicate that organisations like Kids Helpline, Dolly's Dream and Lifeline are likely making a difference. Even so, research indicates there are between 100 and 200 youth suicide attempts for every suicide completed, with child suicide ideation in Australia representing a significant risk factor, as well as prompting family grief and trauma.

Banning social media is unlikely to be the critical initiative that dramatically impacts teen suicide figures in a positive way, however. And 146 specialist organisations and researchers (including me) supported an open letter released by the Australian Child Rights Taskforce in October 2024 arguing that safety standards should instead be imposed on digital platforms alongside 'a focus on supporting and empowering children, families and carers'. There are also indications that social media engagement can be protective for the specific groups of young people at statistically greater risk of self-harm and suicide, including groups identified by the eSafety Commissioner as being at risk of unintended consequences from the social media ban: 'cohorts like LGBTIQ+ teens, First Nations teens and those with disability'.[31]

While there is an understandable focus on cyberbullying, it is only one of the potential harms to teenagers facilitated by digital media. Others include exposure to online hate speech, algorithms and recommender systems, mis- and disinformation, scams, gambling-like content via loot boxes in games, and some aspects of online dating. Teens who are overly concerned with projecting a particular public persona, and who may have body image issues or be over-invested in 'likes', are also at risk of negative impacts. While the Alannah & Madeline Foundation's eSmart Digital Licence+ program addresses and mitigates many of these risks for younger children, their follow-on program, the eSmart Media Literacy Lab, deals with these issues more centrally for secondary-school students. Government support means this program, which helps develop critical thinking in twelve- to sixteen-year-olds, is available to all Australian schools free of cost. Continuing digital literacy education, disengaging overnight and not having connected media in bedrooms, open communication with a trusted adult, and a clear idea of how to access teen-focused, confidential support through targeted online and phone helplines and services can all help mitigate the risks posed by digital media.

But to focus unduly on risks over benefits is to misrepresent the value of digital engagement for teens in their adolescent years. For many children, digital lives are an important point of balance amid the growing pressures of school and their concerns about the state of the world. Young people's digital connections can support the ways in which they carve a future for themselves. Many teens choose to make their online community an extension of, and a deepening of, their offline community. As parents reading may know from personal experience, the bonds forged online and off in these early teen years can provide the social bedrock for an entire lifetime.

Online community takes many forms, and almost all of them can be irksome for parents because they get in the way of family life. If a teen is part of a gaming community, say, it's worth getting to know the parameters of that game. Is it a collaborative team game, with a limited number of players and with each teen having a key role? If so, celebrate the fact that this experience is building valuable skills of mutual trust, specialisation, negotiation and reliability. It's a way for teens to be social, relax, have fun and deepen friendships. If the team is playing competitively, and a game takes on average between forty-five minutes and an hour, it's important to know the impact of calling a team member out of a game to come to, for example, help out with a task that has just arisen—sometimes a team is 'punished' under the rules if a member withdraws. Not only does the team forfeit its game, but players may also be banned from the competition for a period of time, and when the team does re-enter, it starts lower on the ladder than it left. That's a high price for a child to pay in terms of their responsibility to their friendship group.

Regular family discussion as a gaming career develops means these pitfalls can be comparatively easy to avoid. An adult can check in to say that dinner will be at a certain time: 'Can you plan to be clear then?' Or a child can be encouraged to ask: 'Y's suggesting a game. Is it okay if I hop online for an hour?' Such strategies add 'time management skills' to the many other benefits of this kind of gameplay.

Among the decisions that parents make when weighing the pros and cons of adopting a non-interventionist interest in their kids' online lives—since this kind of interest is most likely to keep communication channels open—is the inevitable clash between the bedtime rule, the connected-media-in-the-bedroom rule and the everyday reality of 'I'm just finishing my homework'.

Parents whose family agreements prioritise no connected media in bedrooms tell me that there comes a point, often towards the upper end of this thirteen-to-fifteen age group, where they go to bed before their child, leaving them to finish a game or homework on their laptop in a shared family space, before the teen leaves it and their phone to charge overnight. It's at this stage that keen gamers might start negotiating for a powerful desktop computer, built for gaming, in their bedroom. Among the typical arguments is that it takes up a lot of space in a family area and should not be used by siblings and visitors who might disrupt the settings.

Such requests might prompt a revision, or at least a discussion, of the family technology plan, and whether it is still the best way to prepare your teen to be an online adult with a legal right to access and evaluate all digital content not explicitly banned by law. Faced with similar requests, parents have been known to agree to changes within a range of parameters, such as: phones and portable media remain outside the bedroom; the gaming computer is turned off when the child goes to sleep; the child funds the computer themselves—and contributes towards the cost of faster broadband if that's another of their requests. I believe that these negotiations offer a means through which children have an incentive to learn the costs and responsibilities of adult digital engagement in a supportive environment.

Another hurdle parents negotiate is how fiercely to police the age range classifications for the various games their child (and their child's friends) play online. While parents may be comparatively relaxed about classifications for films and television programs, they often feel pressured by media stories about violent videogames leading to violent behaviour in teens. Despite decades of research, there is no proven causal link between violent media content and any increase in violent behaviour. Instead, parents asking why a teen wants to play a specific game, and maybe declining to buy or supply a game that is not indicated for their child's age group, may be a sufficient means of registering parental reluctance without issuing an outright ban that draws too confrontational a line in the sand.

Instead of being a gamer, your child might be drawn to one or more of the burgeoning online fandoms. While some parents may recall their own experiences of Potterdom with excruciating clarity, these collaborative spaces offer important avenues for self-discovery, identity play and, maybe, creative writing. Teens, often with a core group of friends, co-create and consume fan-based fantasy worlds in which their chosen icons act out a variety of possible (sometimes sexual) futures, helping build skills in empathy and the interpretation of others. As with gamers, the self-organising nature of these communities can astound outsiders. Often, the more established members support new members, and there are proto-classification and content-warning systems for much user-created fan fiction and fan imagery so readers know what to expect from the content they engage with. For many teens who struggle with what they see as social norms, or live with a disability, or are neurodivergent, or identify as a member of the queer community, these fandoms can provide powerful affirmation, significant support and relevant information.

Some parents of teens in this age bracket aren't worrying about their child's digital media use. Instead, they're struggling to manage their child's illegal or life-limiting behaviours, possibly including alcohol, drugs, vaping, smoking, violence, unsafe sex, susceptibility to controlling behaviours and predators, theft and property damage. While some of these risks have a cyber dimension, the child's digital engagement is usually only one element in the precipitating crisis. Many such parents would willingly exchange their own concerns for feeling worried about a teen spending too much time online.

As Catherine Page Jeffery notes, 'parent/adolescent conflict is hardly new', yet digital media gets the blame 'for a growing number of family issues and conflicts'.[32] If your teen is generally open, communicative, engaged in family life, has friends and is focused on creating a positive future, the chances are that all is well. What seems like an online addiction, or an unhealthy preoccupation with one aspect or other of digital culture, is likely a sign of a well-adjusted teen in the second quartile of the twenty-first century.

Australian parents who are interested in what might be termed the general sexual experiences of young people their child's age can refer to La Trobe University's National Survey of Australian Secondary Students and Sexual Health, funded by the Department of Health and Aged Care (SSASH). The most recent is the seventh survey, featuring responses from young people who were fourteen to eighteen years old in 2021. The survey is neither random nor representative: almost two in three of the survey's 6841 participants identified as female, with an average age of 16.2 years. Just under 70 per cent had been, at some point, in a romantic or sexual relationship, with first sexual experiences reported at an average age of fifteen. Forty per cent of the respondent group identified as 'lesbian, gay, bisexual, unsure or used another term (other than heterosexual/straight) to identify their sexuality'. In this study cohort, 86.3 per cent of respondents had received sexual messages or images, with 70.6 per cent saying they had sent them. These figures are indicative.

While young people acknowledge that sending sexual messages is risky, they also argue there are positive aspects to sexting, 'such as learning about their own, and their partner's, sexuality'.[33] The survey doesn't record the average age of first sexting but more respondents report sexting than being, or having ever been, in a romantic or sexual relationship. Sexting seems to be a preliminary step towards a romantic or sexual teen relationship. In effect, as with many adults, teens may use digital intimacy as a starting point for developing trust with a partner before moving onto physical intimacy. Unfortunately, as Australian teens know, when under eighteens sext, they run more risks, and have fewer safeguards, than when adults sext. This is partly because sexual images of people under eighteen can be classified as child sexual abuse material, even when created within a consensual relationship with a same-aged partner and not shared.

Teens' sexts involve legal, financial, health, educational and sociosexual risks. More than 95 per cent of SSASH respondents agreed with the statement 'You have to be careful about sexting' and almost 92 per cent agreed that 'Sending photos may have serious negative consequences'.[34] The sense that teens are 'in the wrong' when they sext can have a chilling effect when it comes to teens reporting image-based sexual harassment and abuse—they worry that others may say the abuse is 'their fault', because they created and sent the sexual image. A similar dynamic also increases fears around teens reporting sextortion. Both the eSafety

Commissioner and the Australian Centre to Counter Child Exploitation offer reassurance and help in these circumstances, with takedown powers and investigation and possible criminal charges against perpetrators, supporting young people and their families in reporting digital image-related aggression, including AI deepfake pornography and other fabricated sexual imagery.

In many ways, the digital and sexual issues that challenge teens in these years are very similar to the ones they tackle in the sixteen-to-eighteen age group. The main differences are that they are still below the age of sexual consent and they are still too young for some social media accounts.

SIXTEEN TO EIGHTEEN

As a child transitions into adulthood, a parent's years of combining careful planning and active listening with collaborative discussion should make these final digital parenting years the least fraught—as far as a child's media use is concerned.

Even so, a few parents may find themselves worrying that their child has become radicalised, or has in other ways adopted an extremist, and sometimes anti-social, ideology. Such concerns will often focus on young men. The eSafety Commissioner has invested in a two-part project looking at the challenges facing young Australian males and notes that 'holding men to account for the harms they cause is central to addressing gender inequity and gender-based violence in Australia'. Part 1 of the project is based on interviews and qualitative research with 117 young men; Part 2 interrogates the perspectives of experts who work to support those 'young men feeling defensive, disenfranchised and uncertain about how to behave'. Such factors may predispose people to be 'responsive to online content, creators and communities that are based on harmful ideas about what it means to be a man'. Practitioners also observed that 'algorithms and recommender systems play a significant role in promoting these harmful ideas'.

One of the findings of this project is heartening: 'boys and men are eager to talk about their issues. They are only waiting for people to listen to them without any judgement and to show they really care.' This is the same kind of connection encouraged in relation to all digital media use—expressing curiosity and interest, asking questions, offering support for the teen through issues arising—basically, avoiding closing down the conversation and enforcing non-negotiable rules. As Daniel Principe notes: 'I genuinely think it is this insecurity … So many boys are not doing as well as girls. And there's people who are documenting this in different ways when it comes to work and school and university achievements. And so, they do feel disenfranchised, and they feel that they're carrying the weight of the privileges of past generations.' Fortunately, the practitioners cited have a range of proven methods for connecting with and supporting young men, including taking a strengths-based approach, and celebrating young men and boys for what they do well.[35]

For most families, however, the period between the sixteenth and eighteenth birthday is when many young people begin to live more autonomous lives, while balancing work, family, friends and (sometimes) intimate relationships. A teen may have had weekend or holiday work for some time and, in many states and territories, sixteen may be the starting point for a future driver's licence, a gateway to more freedom and autonomy. New opportunities and responsibilities—including at school and work, and in romantic contexts—expand young people's horizons, introducing a range of activities that compete with, as well as complement, digital media use. In their book *Parenting for a Digital Future*, Sonia Livingstone and Alicia Blum-Ross meet a mother who is worried about her son's digital media use and ask her 'the critical questions': 'Is he happy?' 'Are his school grades good?' 'Does he have friends?' This mum 'answered "Yes" reluctantly',[36] as if she *wanted* to worry. Livingstone and Blum-Ross focus instead on the positives, which is a good reminder for us all. This is the age when your child becomes a digital adult. Having practised a holistic, engaged parenting style, parents have every reason to hope that their newly minted fully fledged citizen is primed to thrive.

THE DIGITAL CHILD BECOMES A DIGITAL ADULT

Those parents I have spoken to who see their digital parenting journey as complete generally wish they'd been more receptive to their child's perspective and more collaborative around finding compromises. Some parents have regretted being too strict, such as by confiscating phones, saying they did not fully realise the impact of this or how long it would take their child to trust them again. Other parents talk about the sheer exhaustion they felt in trying to monitor everything their child did online. They wish they'd made more time to simply sit and talk with their child about what was happening in their kid's life, their passions and their digital world.

Policy settings that focus on everything that can go wrong digitally get in the way of children moving forward towards a competent, confident digital adulthood. Instead, the village that supports the adult, as well as helping raise the child—the policymakers, educators and government-funded authorities, other parents and the child's friendship networks—should affirm the aspects of digital parenting that can help everything go right: care, compassion and connection. Listening is a transformative superpower, alongside an abiding interest in the who, what and why of a young person's life—online, and off.

ACKNOWLEDGEMENTS

This book encapsulates some twenty-four years of Australian Research Council–funded work for projects with parents, children and their families around everyday digital media use from birth to adulthood. I am privileged to be a Chief Investigator with the ARC Centre of Excellence for the Digital Child (CE200100022) and to co-lead an ARC Discovery Project on 'Teen-Informed Strategies to Counter Sexual Image Abuse and Sextortion' (DP250102379) and an ARC Linkage Project on 'Working with Teens to Co-design a Porn Literacy Program that Mitigates Harm' (LP250100343). My ARC research is implicated in all you read here, so my first big thank-you is to the Australian Research Council, and to my academic home, Edith Cowan University, especially the School of Arts and Humanities.

I'm grateful for a writing retreat run by Dr Sally Knowles at which I planned this book. The London School of Economics and Political Science and my hosts there, Professor Sonia Livingstone and the Digital

Futures for Children research centre, invited me to be a Visiting Scholar for three months in 2025 while I was drafting this manuscript. At Monash University Publishing I'm indebted to Series Curator Greg Bain for offering this opportunity; Publisher Julia Carlomagno for her support, enthusiasm and editorial input; and Marketing Coordinator Sarah Cannon. My family and stepfamily—husband Arthur Hanlon; children Carmen, Benedict, Jim and Claire; and their interested partners and friends—have all informed this work. Indeed, Arthur, Ben and Claire worked with me on the manuscript and made specific suggestions. I also learn from my grandchildren on a near daily basis: thank you, Blaise, Lara, Leander and Robin!

I am especially grateful to my colleagues and collaborators, particularly those working as ethnographers and researchers on the ARC projects, including Ashley Donkin, Belinda Genovese, Birgitta Puspita, Carmen Jacques, Donell Holloway, Emma Jayakumar, Francesca Stocco, Gianfranco Polizzi, Giselle Woodley, Harrison See, Kelly Jaunzems, Kylie Stevenson, Leslie Haddon, Lingyue Ding, Sian Tomkinson, Stephanie Milford, Svenja Ottovordemgentschenfelde and Viet Tho Le. This book would not exist without their help, and without the support of Linda Jaunzems, who has organised me, and my research, since the mid-1990s.

If it takes a village to raise a child, it's taken a generation to create this book. The work would have been impossible without the trust, honesty and sheer generosity of the children, parents, extended family members and friendship groups who welcomed my colleagues and me into their lives and did their best to explain what works for them, and what doesn't, when it comes to young people's digital media use. Thank you all.

KEY RESOURCES

The following resources are discussed in this book and listed in order of appearance.

Expectant parents

ARC Centre of Excellence for the Digital Child, digitalchild.org.au

Young Children in Digital Society, youngchildrendigitalsociety.com.au

Raising Children Network and *Raising Healthy Minds* app, raisingchildren.net.au

Birth to three

Swoosh, Glide and Rule Number 5, eSafety Commissioner, esafety.gov.au/parents/children-under-5/picture-book-and-song/swoosh-glide-and-rule-number-5

Talk Soon. Talk Often. A Guide for Parents Talking to Their Kids 0–18 Years about Relationships and Sex, Western Australian Government, https://tsto.gdhr.wa.gov.au/when-and-how-to-start-talking/sexuality

'Children Under 5', eSafety Commissioner, esafety.gov.au/parents/children-under-5

Four to six

'Finding Balance: Becoming a Screen-Smart Family', Alannah & Madeline Foundation, alannahandmadeline.org.au/learning-resources/digitalk/finding-balance-becoming-a-screen-smart-family

'Family Tech Agreement for Under 5s', eSafety Commissioner, esafety.gov.au/parents/children-under-5/family-tech-agreement-for-under-5s

'A Family Technology Plan: How to Make One', Raising Children Network, raisingchildren.net.au/toddlers/videos/family-technology-plan-how-to-make-one

'Bullying Is Not OK', Kids Helpline, kidshelpline.com.au/kids/issues/bullying-not-ok

'Circle of Friends: Personal Boundaries Activity', Raising Children Network, raisingchildren.net.au/autism/development/sexual-development/circle-of-friends-personal-boundaries-activity-children-3-15-years

Seven to nine

Luna Period Tracker for Teens, lunatracker.app/

'How to Help Your Child Being Cyberbullied', eSafety Commissioner, esafety.gov.au/newsroom/blogs/how-to-help-your-child-being-cyberbullied

'How to Collect Evidence', eSafety Commissioner, esafety.gov.au/report/how-to-collect-evidence

'Counselling and Support', eSafety Commissioner, esafety.gov.au/report/counselling-support

'Gift Guide', eSafety Commissioner, esafety.gov.au/parents/resources/gift-guide

'I Want Help With Being Safe Online', eSafety Kids, esafety.gov.au/kids/I-want-help-with/being-safe-online

'How Do I Know If I Have Been Mean to Others Online', eSafety Kids, esafety.gov.au/kids/I-want-help-with/how-do-i-know-if-im-being-mean-online

'Someone is Contacting Me and I Don't Want Them To', eSafety Kids, esafety.gov.au/kids/I-want-help-with/someone-is-contacting-me-and-i-dont-want-them-to

'How to Talk with Children about Sexting', Raising Children Network, raisingchildren.net.au/pre-teens/entertainment-technology/pornography-sexting/sexting-early-conversations

'Talking to Children about Pornography', Raising Children Network, raisingchildren.net.au/school-age/media-technology/online-safety/pornography-talking-with-children-5-8

'Child Sexual Abuse: Helplines and Services', Raising Children Network, raisingchildren.net.au/pre-teens/mental-health-physical-health/child-sexual-abuse/child-sexual-abuse-helplines-and-services

Ten to twelve

'Being a Young Man Online', esafety.gov.au/sites/default/files/2024-06/Being-a-young-man-online-June-2024.pdf?v=1737763200031

Safety by Design, eSafety Commissioner, esafety.gov.au/industry/safety-by-design

'How to Determine if Your Child Is Ready for Their Own Smartphone', Alannah & Madeline Foundation, alannahandmadeline.org.au/resources/how-to-determine-if-your-child-is-ready-for-their-own-smartphone

Thirteen to fifteen

'When Love Becomes Control', eSafety Commissioner, esafety.gov.au/newsroom/blogs/when-love-becomes-control

ReachOut free online or telephone support for parents, parents.au.reachout.com/one-on-one-support

'Sextortion: What Is It?', Australian Centre for Countering Child Exploitation, accce.gov.au/sextortionhelp

Dolly's Dream, dollysdream.org.au

Beyond Blue Youth Support, beyondblue.org.au/mental-health/youth

ReachOut advice on supporting children and gender identity, parents.au.reachout.com/culture-and-identity/gender

'First Nations: Online Hate and Abuse', eSafety Commissioner, esafety.gov.au/first-nations/online-hate-and-abuse

'Bullying Online', eSafety Commissioner, esafety.gov.au/young-people/cyberbullying

eSmart Media Literacy Lab, alannahandmadeline.org.au/what-we-do/prevention-programs/esmart/media-literacy-lab

eSmart Parents and Caregivers, alannahandmadeline.org.au/what-we-do/prevention-programs/esmart/esmart-parents

National Survey of Australian Secondary Students and Sexual Health, La Trobe University, ssashsurvey.org.au

Sixteen to eighteen

'Supporting Young Men Online', esafety.gov.au/sites/default/files/2025-02/Supporting-young-men-online-report-2.pdf

REFERENCES

Alannah & Madeline Foundation, 'Navigating the 4Cs of Online Safety', eSmart Digital Licence, undated.

Australian Bureau of Statistics, 'Suicide of Children Aged 5–17 Years, 2020–2024', 14 November 2025, abs.gov.au.

Australian Child Rights Taskforce, Open Letter on the Proposed Social Media Ban, 9 October 2024.

Australian Government, 'Response to the House of Representatives Select Committee on Social Media and Online Safety Report', March 2023.

Australian Government, 'Social Media and Online Safety Report', House of Representatives Select Committee on Social Media and Online Safety, March 2022.

Bazalgette, Cary, *How Toddlers Learn the Secret Language of Movies*, Springer, 2022.

eSafety Commissioner, 'Talking About Child Sexual Abuse Online with 0 to 12 Year Olds', 16 January 2026.

Grant, Julie Inman, 'A Way Forward: Disrupting the Darker Forces Impacting Young Men Online', eSafety Commissioner, 4 February 2025.

Grant, Julie Inman, 'Cyberbullying and the Back-to-School Surge: How We Can Protect Our Kids', eSafety Commissioner, 19 February 2025.

Grant, Julie Inman, 'How to Help Your Child Being Cyberbullied', eSafety Commissioner, 27 March 2019.

Grant, Julie Inman, 'Learning from the Past to Safeguard Children's Online Future', eSafety Commissioner, 10 October 2024.

Green, Lelia et al., *Digital Media Use in Early Childhood: Birth to Six*, Bloomsbury, 2024.

Haidt, Jonathan, *The Anxious Generation: How the Great Rewiring of Childhood is Causing an Epidemic of Mental Illness*, Penguin Random House, 2024.

Leaver, Tama Bruno and Sardarov, Suzanne, *Children and Generative AI (GenAI) in Australia: The Big Challenges*, ARC Centre of Excellence for the Digital Child, 2025.

Livingstone, Sonia and Blum-Ross, Alicia, *Parenting for a Digital Future: How Hopes and Fears about Technology Shape Children's Lives*, Oxford University Press, 2020.

Office of the eSafety Commissioner, 'AI Chatbots and Companions—Risks to Children and Young People', 18 February 2025.

Office of the eSafety Commissioner, 'An Unfair Fight—How Algorithms Are Shaping Our Adolescents', 17 April 2025.

Office of the eSafety Commissioner, 'Behind the Screen: The Reality of Age Assurance and Social Media Access for Young Australians—Transparency Report', February 2025.

Osman, Kim et al., 'Young Australians' Perspectives on the Social Media Minimum Age Legislation', Digital Media Research Centre, Queensland University of Technology, 2025.

Page Jeffery, Catherine, *Parenting in a Digital World: Beyond Media Panics Towards a New Theory of Parental Mediation*, Routledge, 2025.

Power, Jennifer et al., *The 7th National Survey of Australian Secondary Students and Sexual Health 2021*, The Australian Research Centre in Sex, Health and Society, La Trobe University, 2022.

Reucassel, Craig, 'What Do Teenagers Think About a Social Media Age Limit?', ABC, 11 October 2024.

Shafer, Ashley E., Wanless, Shannon B. and Briggs, Jennifer O., 'Toddler Teachers' Responses to Tantrums and Relations to Successful Resolutions', *Infant and Child Development*, vol. 31, no. 3, 2022, e2304.

Suicide Prevention Australia, 'Stats and Facts', 2024.

Turvey, Jake, McKay, Dana, Kaur, Sarah T., Castree, Natasha, Chang, Shanton and Lim, Megan S.C., 'Exploring the Feasibility and Acceptability of Technological Interventions to Prevent Adolescents' Exposure to Online Pornography: Qualitative Research', *JMIR Pediatrics and Parenting*, vol. 7, 2024, e58684.

Wisbey, Michelle, 'Girls' Periods Starting Earlier and More Irregular: Study', *NewsGP*, 31 May 2024.

Woodley, Giselle Natassia, Green, Lelia and Jacques, Carmen, 'Send Nudes?': Teens' Perspectives of Education Around Sexting, An Argument for a Balanced Approach', *Sexualities*, vol. 28, no. 5–6, pp. 1891–1909.

NOTES

1 Grant, 'Learning from the Past to Safeguard Children's Online Future'.
2 Stephen Graham and Jack Thorne, *Adolescence* (dir. Philip Barantini), Netflix, 2025.
3 Misia Temler, 'It's Tempting to Offload Your Thinking to AI. Cognitive Science Shows Why That's a Bad Idea', *The Conversation*, 10 March 2026 and Sarah Whitcombe-Dobbs, 'Why Exposing Young Children to AI Content Could Have Irreversible Consequences', *The Conversation*, 13 March 2026.
4 Livingstone and Blum-Ross, *Parenting for a Digital Future*, p. 194.
5 'Five Key Findings from a Study on Parents' Experiences of Infant Feeding and Baby-Tracking Apps', Digital Child, December 2024, and 'Five Key Things to Understand: Sharing Photos of Your Child Online', Digital Child, February 2025.
6 Ned Potter, 'To A Baby, A Magazine Is "An iPad That Does Not Work"', ABC News, 2011.
7 Green et al., *Digital Media Use in Early Childhood*, pp. 124, 132.
8 Cary Bazalgette, *How Toddlers Learn the Secret Language of Movies*, Springer, 2022.

9 Shafer et al., 'Toddler Teachers' Responses to Tantrums and Relations to Successful Resolutions', p. 15.
10 *Talk Soon. Talk Often.* Western Australian Government, https://tsto.gdhr.wa.gov.au/when-and-how-to-start-talking/sexuality
11 Green et al., *Digital Media Use in Early Childhood*, pp. 148–49.
12 Wisbey, 'Girls' Periods Starting Earlier and More Irregular'.
13 Grant, 'Learning from the Past to Safeguard Children's Online Future'.
14 Grant, 'How to Help Your Child Being Cyberbullied'.
15 eSafety Commissioner, 'Talking About Child Sexual Abuse Online with 0 to 12 Year Olds'.
16 Alannah & Madeline Foundation, 'Navigating the 4Cs of Online Safety'.
17 Woodley et al., 'Send Nudes?', pp. 1891–1909.
18 Leaver & Sardarov, *Children and Generative AI (GenAI) in Australia*.
19 Grant, 'Cyberbullying and the Back-to-School Surge'.
20 Grant, 'Learning from the Past to Safeguard Children's Online Future'.
21 'The Social Media Ban for Under 16's: Staying Informed', headspace, 29 November 2024.
22 Grant, 'A Way Forward'.
23 'AI Chatbots and Companions—Risks to Children and Young People', eSafety Commissioner, 18 February 2025.
24 Turvey et al., 'Exploring the Feasibility and Acceptability of Technological Interventions to Prevent Adolescents' Exposure to Online Pornography'.
25 Emma McGrath-Cohen & Tess Bennett, 'Fines Loom for Social Media Giants as Kids Give Ban 100-Day Fail Mark', *Australian Financial Review*, 19 March 2026.
26 Osman et al., 'Young Australians' Perspectives on the Social Media Minimum Age Legislation'.

27 Graham, Jackson, 'We're Teenagers, We're Going to Rebel': The Families Yet to See the Social Media Ban Work', *The Sydney Morning Herald*, 20 March 2026.
28 Suicide Prevention Australia, 'Stats and Facts', 2024.
29 Grant, 'Learning from the Past to Safeguard Children's Online Future'.
30 ABS, 'Suicide of Children Aged 5–17 Years, 2020–2024'.
31 Grant, 'Learning from the Past to Safeguard Children's Online Future'.
32 Page Jeffery, *Parenting in a Digital World*, p. 82.
33 Power et al., p. 12.
34 Power et al., p. 71.
35 'Supporting Young Men Online', eSafety Commissioner, February 2025, pp. 22, 63.
36 Livingstone and Blum-Ross, *Parenting for a Digital Future*, p. 98.

IN THE NATIONAL INTEREST

Other books on the issues that matter:

Esther Anatolitis *When Australia Became a Republic*
David Anderson *Now More than Ever: Australia's ABC*
Kevin Bell *Housing: The Great Australian Right*
Bill Bowtell *Unmasked: The Politics of Pandemics*
Michael Bradley *System Failure: The Silencing of Rape Survivors*
Melissa Castan & Lynette Russell *Time to Listen: An Indigenous Voice to Parliament*
Inala Cooper *Marrul: Aboriginal Identity & the Fight for Rights*
Kim Cornish *The Post-Pandemic Child*
Samantha Crompvoets *Blood Lust, Trust & Blame*
Satyajit Das *Fortune's Fool: Australia's Choices*
Richard Denniss *Big: The Role of the State in the Modern Economy*
Rachel Doyle *Power & Consent*
Jo Dyer *Burning Down the House: Reconstructing Modern Politics*
Wayne Errington & Peter van Onselen *Who Dares Loses: Pariah Policies*
Gareth Evans *Good International Citizenship: The Case for Decency*
Paul Farrell *Gladys: A Leader's Undoing*
Kate Fitz-Gibbon *Our National Crisis: Violence against Women & Children*
Kate Fitz-Gibbon *Our National Shame: Violence against Women*
Paul Fletcher *Governing in the Internet Age*
Carrillo Gantner *Dismal Diplomacy, Disposable Sovereignty: Our Problem with China & America*
Paula Gerber *Sex, Gender & Identity: Trans Rights in Australia*
Quentin Grafton *Retelling Australia's Water Story*
Matthew Harding *Charities & Politics: A Principled Approach*
Jill Hennessy *Respect*

(continued from previous page)

Lucinda Holdforth *21st-Century Virtues: How They Are Failing Our Democracy*

Simon Holmes à Court *The Big Teal*

Bryan Horrigan *Corporate Social Responsibility in an Age of Existential Threats*

Andrew Jaspan & Lachlan Guselli *The Consultancy Conundrum: The Hollowing Out of the Public Sector*

Andrew Leigh *Fair Game: Lessons from Sport for a Fairer Society & a Stronger Economy*

Ian Lowe *Australia on the Brink: Avoiding Environmental Ruin*

John Lyons *Dateline Jerusalem: Journalism's Toughest Assignment*

Richard Marles *Tides that Bind: Australia in the Pacific*

Fiona McLeod *Easy Lies & Influence*

Michael Mintrom *Advancing Human Rights*

Louise Newman *Rape Culture*

Martin Parkinson *A Decade of Drift*

Jennifer Rayner *Climate Clangers: The Bad Ideas Blocking Real Action*

Isabelle Reinecke *Courting Power: Law, Democracy & the Public Interest in Australia*

Abul Rizvi *Population Shock*

Richard Royle & David Hansen *Connected Care: Digital Health in Australia*

Kevin Rudd *The Case for Courage*

Don Russell *Leadership*

Scott Ryan *Challenging Politics*

Ronli Sifris *Towards Reproductive Justice*

Kate Thwaites & Jenny Macklin *Enough Is Enough*

Graeme Turner *Broken: Universities, Politics & the Public Good*

Simon Wilkie *The Digital Revolution: A Survival Guide*

Carla Wilshire *Time to Reboot: Feminism in the Algorithm Age*

Campbell Wilson *Living with AI*

Thom Woodroofe *Power, Prosperity & Planet: Climate and Energy Policy for All*